Jumpin' Johnny
GET BACK TO WORK!

A Child's Guide to ADHD/Hyperactivity

Michael Gordon, Ph.D.
Professor, Department of Psychiatry
Director, ADHD Program
SUNY Health Science Center at Syracuse

Illustrations and design
Janet Junco

GSI Publications, Inc.
P.O. Box 746, DeWitt, NY. 13214
1-800-550-ADHD Fax: (315) 446-2012
Visit our web site at http://www.gsi-add.com

PUBLICATIONS, INC.

SPECIAL THANKS

To Drs. Russell A. Barkley, Ruth C. Burton, Harvey C. Parker and Wendy E. Gordon for reviewing the manuscript. I also very much appreciate the editorial assistance offered by my junior staff: P.J. Corrigan, Jason Conner, Joshua Gordon, Alexander Gordon, and Seth Downen. -M.G.

ABOUT THE ILLUSTRATOR

A graduate of Carnegie-Mellon University, Janet Junco has worked as a graphic designer for the N.Y.S. Department of Health and then for the SUNY Health Science Center at Syracuse, NY. In 1987 she was the recipient of two Nori Awards for her wall poster and public relations campaign designed for a public policy conference on AIDS.

ISBN# 0-9627701-1-6

GSI Publications, Inc.
P.O. Box 746, DeWitt, NY. 13214
1-800-550-ADHD Fax: (315) 446-2012
Visit our web site at http://www.gsi-add.com

PUBLICATIONS, INC.

F O R E W O R D

You're about to read a story about a boy who has trouble paying attention and keeping still even when he really tries. Along with his family and teacher, he finds that he has an Attention Deficit Hyperactivity Disorder (ADHD). You'll see how everyone involved learns to cope with his handicap.

This book was written for ADHD youngsters who want to understand how their problem was identified and what kinds of feelings and concerns they might experience throughout the process of evaluation and treatment. You will notice that no attempt has been made to sugarcoat or romanticize the life of an ADHD child. The story is told by a youngster who truly struggles to achieve, but doesn't always meet with success or acceptance. Although he moves through the day experiencing frustration and embarrassment, he still maintains his sense of humor and spirit of determination.

While "Jumpin' Johnny" was intended to help ADHD children learn about their problem, you might well find that brothers, sisters, friends, and classmates would benefit from the opportunity to gain insight into the nature of this disorder. After all, ADHD children can use all the understanding that their world can muster. Fortunately for the Jumpin' Johnnys (and Janeys) of the world, small doses of compassion can produce powerful and longlasting effects.

Harvey C. Parker, Ph.D.
Founder, Children with Attention Deficit Disorders (CH.A.D.D.)
National Support Group

I just got yelled at again. It wasn't the first time today. It wasn't even the fifth. Maybe the tenth. It probably won't be the last time either.

This has not been a very good day. I forgot my lunch bag even though my Mom had just reminded me to put it in my backpack. Now I'll have to beg Jeremy for a half of his jelly sandwich. Last time that cost me three baseball cards.

I tried to get these stupid math sheets done when Mrs. Arrow said. I rushed through them as fast as I could because I wanted to be the first one to play on the computer. But I hurried so much that I got the pluses and minuses all mixed up. I had to do the whole dumb thing over again.

Then Mrs. Arrow said that the paper was too messy and, you got it, back to my desk to do it over. I never did make it to the computer.

The thing is that I really want to do well. But everyone thinks I'm just plain lazy. Or maybe dumb and lazy.

I admit it. I do squirm around in my seat a lot and drum my pencil on the desk. Mrs. Arrow doesn't like it when I wriggle. She's always saying, "Stop jumping, Johnny, and get back to work!" That's why the kids all call me "Jumpin' Johnny."

Just yesterday Melissa said, "Jumpin' Johnny, get back to work!" Everybody giggled but me.

I'll just be sitting there and, without thinking, I start unwinding the thread on my sleeve or tapping my foot against the chair. I guess I like to be moving because it keeps me more awake and interested.

But I really don't try to upset anyone. That's the part that I don't think the grownups understand. Even when I really try hard, I can't pay attention and finish my work as well as the other kids.

It's sort of like half of my brain tells me to pay attention while the other half tries to get me to check what's happening in the hallway or out the window. And looking out the window at the birds is a heck of a lot more interesting than most of this school work. You know, if I have to do one more pile of these dittos, I think I'm going to scream until I can scream no more.

I sure don't like people being upset with me. Not long ago I heard my mother crying. The teacher had called to tell her about my bad grades. Of course, she also mentioned about how I hadn't watched where I was going in the cafeteria and knocked two food trays over. It didn't help much that it had been spaghetti day.

It bothers me a lot when my parents get so unhappy with me. I wish I knew how to tell them how I feel. Or that I'm sorry. Whenever I try, I don't know what to say and I feel yucky all over.

Something awful happened last week. My Dad found the antenna broken on his new radio and asked me if I was the one who did it. Dad always asks me first when something gets messed up because I'm usually the one who's not as careful as I should be. Without even thinking, I told him that I had nothing to do with the radio. But I knew that wasn't true. I just didn't want to get into trouble again. I'm tired of getting into trouble.

Boy, that ended up being a big mistake. I wish I had thought a little more about what would happen when my Dad found out the truth. Who told him? My sister, Little Miss Wonderful. If there were a deep hole you could bury cute little sisters in without getting into trouble, I would have done it long ago.

TURN
OFF
LIGHTS

I was embarrassed the other day because I was taken out of the class by this man the teacher told me was the school psychologist. I didn't want to go because I was afraid that the other kids would make fun of me. All I needed was for them to tease me even more than they already did. They always tell me I'm crazy and stupid. And what would happen if the psychologist found out that I really was crazy and stupid?

It turned out that the psychologist was a pretty nice guy and the tests weren't too hard. You had to copy these designs and there were some puzzles and math problems. Stuff like that.

Then my Mom, Dad and I went to a special doctor who was good at working with children who have trouble paying attention. At first I was worried about getting shots

or having to take my clothes off and get tickled. But this was a different kind of doctor. He was more of a talking doctor.

Boy, did he ask questions! About school and friends and family and worries and why getting my work done was so hard. He also had me take these tests where I had to pay attention for what seemed like forever. Actually, it was pretty cool because it was all done on this special computer.

When the questions and tests were all finished, the doctor explained to me and my parents that I have a problem called "Attention Deficit Hyperactivity Disorder" or ADHD for short. It's what they call what happens when you can't pay attention even when you really try. The doctor said that lots of kids have this problem. And it has nothing to do with being dumb or crazy. In fact, he told me that I was one smart cookie. I wish he would make a big sign saying, "Jumpin' Johnny is one smart cookie," and hang it in my classroom for everyone to see.

My Dad told me that I wasn't the first one in our family with ADHD. He said that Uncle Willy had a terrible time in school because he never sat still. Grandpa said that he was like a "bug in a frying pan." Dad said that all the kids would call him "Wigglin' Willy." Maybe that's why Uncle Willy and I get along so well.

Things have started to change. The grownups don't get as angry at me so quickly. My Dad said that it wasn't fair to yell at me if some of what I did wrong wasn't because I was trying to be bad. He said it would be like yelling at a deaf person because they couldn't hear.

But don't worry that my parents forgot how to get annoyed with me. I still get into plenty of trouble that even I can't blame on my ADHD! My Dad said that having ADHD isn't an excuse for misbehaving. But knowing I have ADHD makes them understand how hard it is sometimes for me to behave the way I should.

It was hard to understand how I could be smart and have problems at the same time. And I didn't like everybody talking about me like I had some kind of disease. But my parents explained that many kids have trouble paying attention. They said that I have a great brain, but the part that helps me pay attention doesn't work so well unless things are so interesting that they almost reach out and grab my attention. Like Nintendo.

The best change is that I don't feel like I am some sort of criminal any more. My teacher and I have started to find ways I can learn and get my work done without having so much trouble. She's moved my desk to the front of the room where it's easier for her to help me keep working. She also comes over and checks to make sure that I understand the directions.

We came up with this special program we decided to call "Magic Marbles." Every morning Mrs. Arrow puts 8 marbles in a cup that she puts on my desk. She also taped a piece of paper to the cup with these three rules written on it:

1. No disturbing the class by talking out of turn or getting out of the seat at the wrong time.
2. No work left unfinished because of daydreaming.
3. No sloppy work.

13

I get to keep all the marbles as long as I don't break any of the rules. She takes a marble away if I do break one of the rules. The best part is that each marble is worth 3 minutes on the computer. I try harder at school because I seriously want to play on that computer. "Magic Marbles" makes it more interesting and fun to pay attention.

I have to tell you that at first I was embarrassed about being the only one in the class who did the marble program. But then I figured that it was less embarrassing than being yelled at. I must be doing pretty well with it because all of a sudden Robert and Susan have marble cups on their desks, too. They also have trouble finishing their work.

Mrs. Arrow and I also worked out this secret signal. If I start to look away from my work, she comes by and taps my right shoulder. That quietly reminds me to get back to work.

The best thing Mrs. Arrow has done is to change how much work I have to do. Because it's so hard for me, she's cut back a little bit on the number of pages I have to finish. But I still have to do them just right. Some of the other kids complained that I didn't have to do as much as they did.

Mrs. Arrow really came through on this one. She said that some kids need special arrangements because they learn differently than other children. Like if a child was blind in one eye or was hard of hearing, you would need to make up a special program. And then she told them how I had to work just as hard to get 3 dittos done as they did to get 6 finished. We were all working just as hard but, because of my problem, I needed a smaller assignment.

Not having a mountain of homework assigned made an awesome difference. I used to hate when 4 o'clock came because that's when the homework wars began. I can tell you that the last thing I wanted to do after a horrible day at school was to work on homework all night. Now I know that my work should take me no more than 30 minutes to finish. I can handle that. Of course, if I fool around, it might take me longer. But no more all night misery! It's nice to have some of the pressure off.

Mrs. Arrow also started sending a little sheet home every day to let my parents know what kind of day I had and what needed to be done for homework. I really didn't like that at first because I was afraid I'd be punished at home if I had a bad day. But it has turned out okay. It's just a way for my parents to know how I'm doing so they don't get all worried. It's also good that my parents know what assignments are due so they can help me remember to do them.

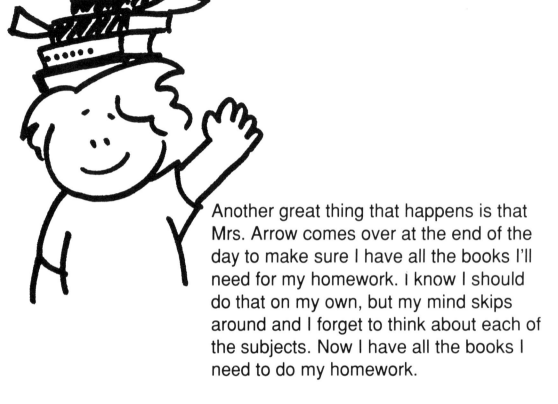

Another great thing that happens is that Mrs. Arrow comes over at the end of the day to make sure I have all the books I'll need for my homework. I know I should do that on my own, but my mind skips around and I forget to think about each of the subjects. Now I have all the books I need to do my homework.

At home, Mom and Dad had these new ideas about doing things so that they wouldn't always have to remind me and yell. It was kind of like a business deal. We decided that I could earn one hour of TV time every day. They used to only let me watch a 1/2 hour, so now I have a chance to see twice as much. (I tried to get them to make it an hour and a half, but they didn't go for it.)

Then we decided on these three rules for my behavior at home:

1.   No forgetting to listen the first time I am asked to do something.
2.   No hitting, kicking or shoving or other aggressive behavior.
3.   No lying.

They have 6 chips and each is worth 10 minutes of TV. As long as I don't break any of the rules I get to keep all the chips and watch a whole hour of TV. But if I mess up and break one of the rules, then I lose a chip.

We also agreed that, if I start arguing about losing a chip, that costs me another chip.

I've learned that I have good days and bad days. Sometimes I get so tired of trying to be good that I slip a bit. This used to bother my Mom and Dad because they'd worry that I was going to have a lot of trouble again. I think they're starting to calm down.

Oops, I almost forgot to tell you about the medicine. At first I thought it was kind of weird to take a pill to help me pay attention. And I was a little nervous about how it would make me feel. But if you think I was nervous about it, you should have seen my parents. They talked to all kinds of doctors and read this big pile of books.

But we decided it was worth trying so that we could see if it helped me. The doctor told me all about the medicine and let me ask some questions. I didn't really know what to ask except I wanted to know if I would be taking drugs you're not supposed to use. Like they show on the commercials when they tell you, "Just Say No."

The doctor said that this medicine wasn't like the bad drugs and was safe to take because he and my parents would be real careful and that we'd work together like a team. He also said I needed to let them know if I had any problems with it. Like if I felt funny or got headaches or stomachaches. And definitely if it made me feel completely weird. He also wanted to know if I thought that it helped me.

To tell you the truth, I don't feel all that different on the medicine, except that I'm not as hungry for lunch. The only thing I see that has changed about me is that my handwriting is better and it's a little easier for me to pay attention to my work at school. And I don't get into quite so much trouble for doing things without thinking first. I hear myself saying to myself, "Are you really sure you should do that?" I didn't used to think much first before I'd do something.

At first I tried to use the medicine for excuses when I'd get into trouble. I'd say something like, "I forgot my hat and gloves in school because you didn't give me enough of my medicine." Boy, that didn't get me far! My Mom said that I am responsible for what I do whether I'm taking the medicine or not. But you can't blame a kid for trying!

So that's the story so far. I can feel that everybody's trying hard and I'm doing my best. Of course, my little sister's still perfect. My Mom didn't like my suggestion that we sell her to another family and use the money to buy a computer game.

Other than Little Miss Wonderful, I think life's okay. I have to tell you, though, that a lot of times I just can't wait until I'm grown up so nobody will tell me, "Jumping Johnny, get back to work!"